CHOIR BUILDERS

Fundamental Vocal Techniques for Classroom and General Use

By Rollo Dilworth

Edited by Janet Day

CONTENTS

HAL•LEONARD®
CORPORATION

7777 W. BLUEMOUND RD. P.O. BOX 13819 MILWAUKEE, WI 53213

Visit Hal Leonard Online at
www.halleonard.com

| | | Piano |
| | Voices | Accompaniment |

PHILOSOPHY AND GOALS

This book is designed with the following goals in mind:

A to foster healthy vocal/choral development for choirs at all levels;
B to facilitate focused singing using unison, 2-part, 3-part, and 4-part textures;
C to prepare choral voices for artistically expressive performance.

To this end, this author has combined the teaching philosophies of Zoltán Kodály (1882-1967), Emile Jacques-Dalcroze (1865-1950), Carl Orff (1895-1982), along with original methodologies, in an effort to synthesize a holistic approach to choral pedagogy addressing the diversity of learning styles that exist in a given rehearsal setting.

HOW TO USE THIS BOOK

This book is divided into the following chapters:

1 Preparatory Exercises
2 Vocal Exercises – Unison
3 Vocal Exercises – Unison with Optional 2-part
4 Vocal Exercises – 2-part Treble or Mixed
5 Vocal Exercises – 3-part or 4-part Mixed
■ Piano Accompaniments
■ Appendix

PREPARATORY EXERCISES
The Preparatory Exercises are designed to prepare the body for singing. In addition to the posture exercise that introduces the unit, there are 96 patterns that have been constructed to facilitate controlled breathing, rhythmic accuracy and stability, good diction (attacks, sustained vowels, and releases), and activation of the head voice. These Rhythm Calisthenics are to be performed by the teacher/leader then echoed back by the singers. The pages of the patterns can be copied onto heavy paper and then cut into individual cards. The cards can be performed in sequence or in random order. Feel free to alter the patterns (rhythms, consonants, vowels, etc.) to suit the needs of your ensemble.

VOCAL EXERCISES
All Vocal Exercises (unison, 2-part, 3-part, and 4-part) are designed to address two or more musical concepts at once. An instruction guide that contains the following information supports each warm-up activity:

FOCAL POINTS   outlines the key concepts to be addressed by the warm-up activity.

EXPLANATION   provides instruction on how to use the warm-up exercise.

EXPANSION   offers ideas for varying the performance of the warm-up exercise, including tempo, dynamics, articulations, style, use of Multiple Expression Levels (M.E.L.) See appendix for guide.

EXTENSION   offers ideas for expanding the warm-up exercise to include other content areas (solfege, movement, hand signs, National Music Education Standards).

PIANO ACCOMPANIMENTS
Piano accompaniments for all vocal exercises are provided. The accompanist is invited to improvise and/or modulate beyond the range of the vocal exercise if desired.

Piano accompaniment pages are cross referenced on each exercise.

Page #

Exercise pages are cross referenced on each piano accompaniment page.

Page #

APPENDIX
The appendix includes the following helpful guides:
- Multiple Expression Levels (M.E.L.)
- Kodály/Curwen Hand Signs
- Kodály Rhythm Syllables
- National Standards for Music Education
- Basic Conducting Patterns

FROM THE PUBLISHER
The flexible set-up of this book allows you to use this resource in a variety of ways:

- Use for large or small group warm-ups.
- Start at the beginning and work your way to the end or,
- Choose a song from each chapter every rehearsal or,
- Choose exercises on the topic your choir needs the most help and concentrate on those.
- The original purchaser of this book has permission to reproduce any of the exercises for educational use only. Any other use is strictly prohibited. Many of the exercises may be taught by rote, but for some of the more challenging divisi warm-ups, you may choose to give each choir member a copy of the exercise.
- Note there are no dynamics or tempo markings throughout. The director should choose the tempo that works best for the group's level of proficiency. Vary the dynamics as you see fit. The enclosed CD should serve as a guide.
- The accompaniments are meant to enhance the exercises. However, if you choose to modulate in a different direction than the accompaniment or for more repetitions than the accompaniment, feel free to sing the exercise a cappella or if your accompanist can continue with the modulations, keep modulating upward or downward as needed.
- Use the CD included for a "hands-free" warm-up, a student-directed warm-up, or a transportable warm-up for off-site performances/rehearsals. The track numbers are indicated throughout.

Track #

However you choose to utilize this book, may it offer useful songs and exercises for optimal choir building!

CHAPTER 1

PREPARATION

Posture Perfect!

While in a standing position with feet slightly apart (about even with the shoulders),
chant this rap to become posture perfect for singing!

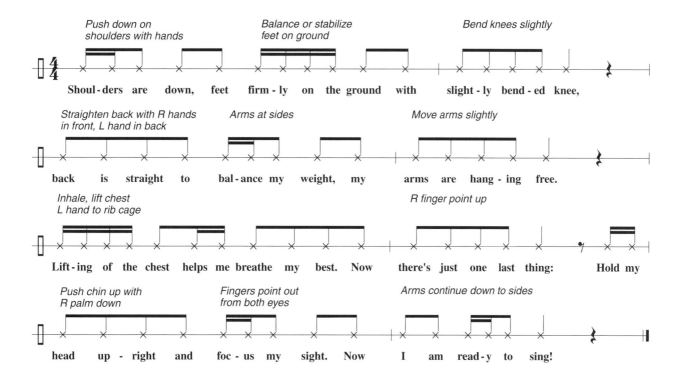

Push down on shoulders with hands   *Balance or stabilize feet on ground*   *Bend knees slightly*

Shoul-ders are down, feet firm-ly on the ground with slight-ly bend-ed knee,

Straighten back with R hands in front, L hand in back   *Arms at sides*   *Move arms slightly*

back is straight to bal-ance my weight, my arms are hang-ing free.

Inhale, lift chest L hand to rib cage   *R finger point up*

Lift-ing of the chest helps me breathe my best. Now there's just one last thing: Hold my

Push chin up with R palm down   *Fingers point out from both eyes*   *Arms continue down to sides*

head up-right and foc-us my sight. Now I am read-y to sing!

Rhythm Calisthenics – see page iii for directions.

PREPARATION

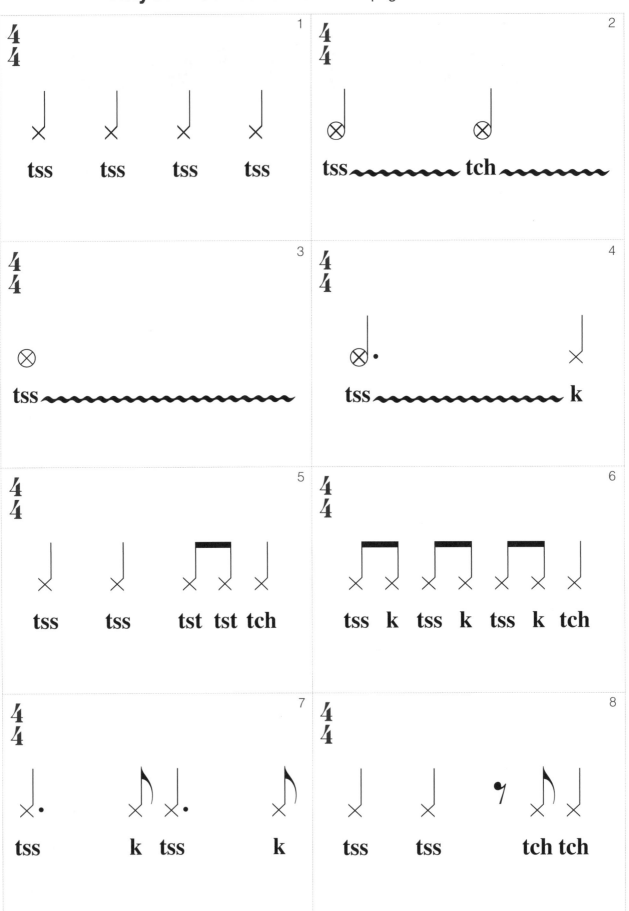

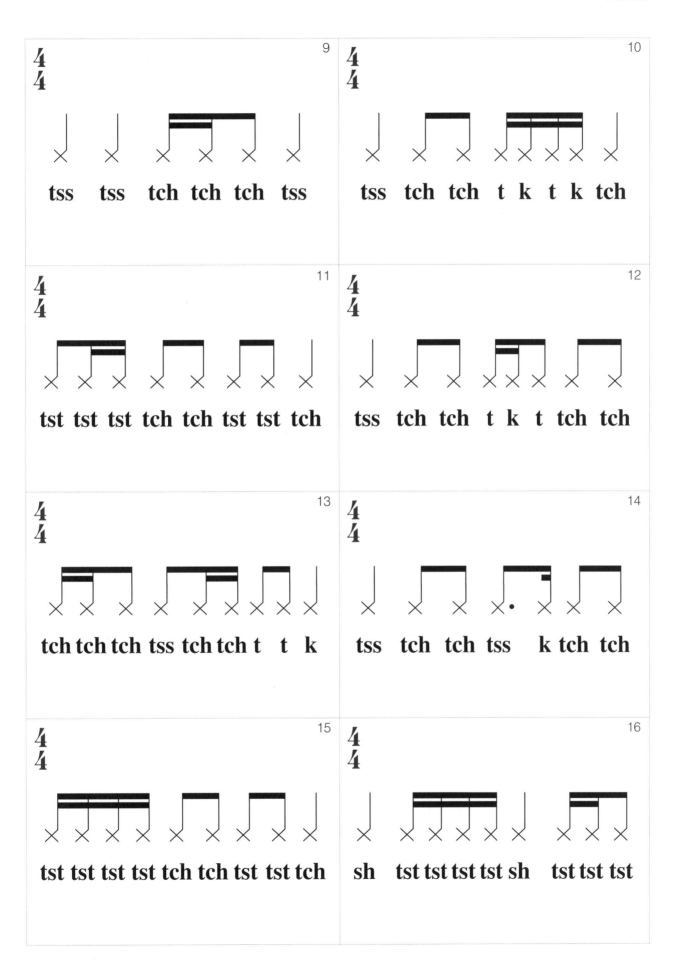

PREPARATION

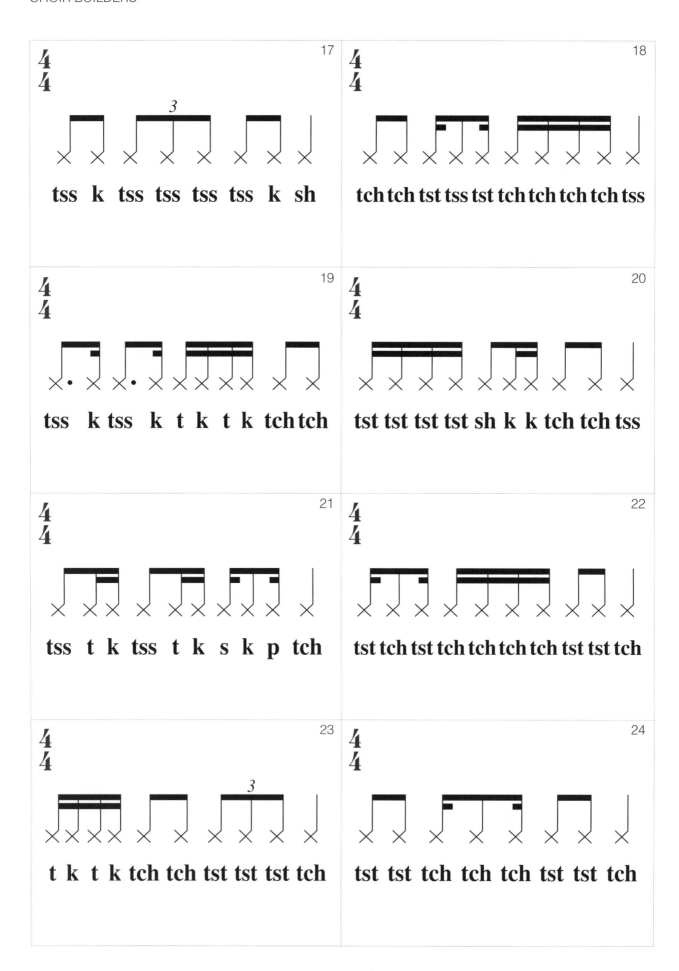

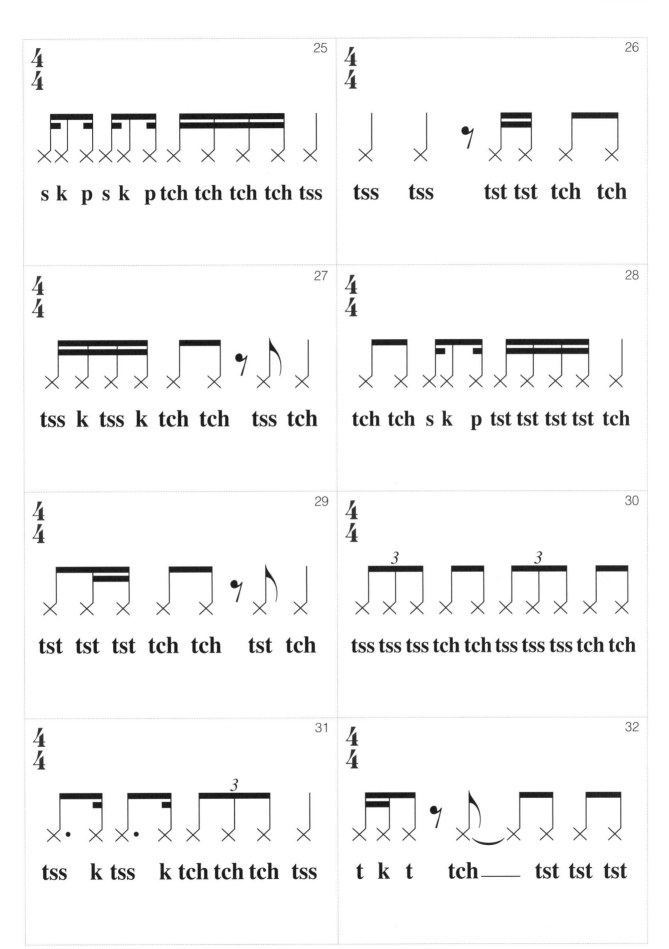

PREPARATION

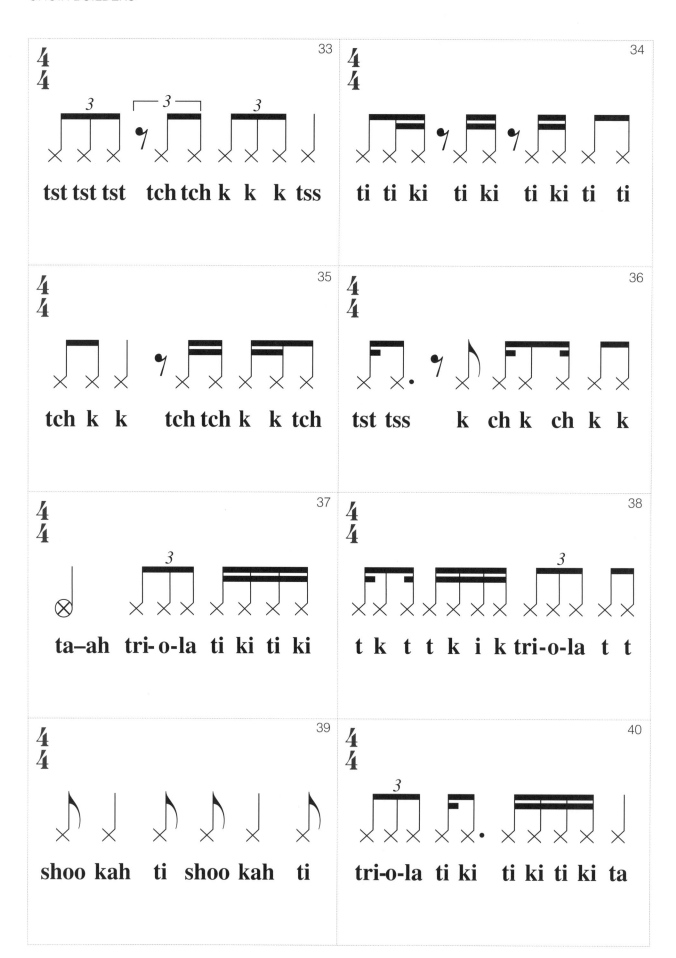

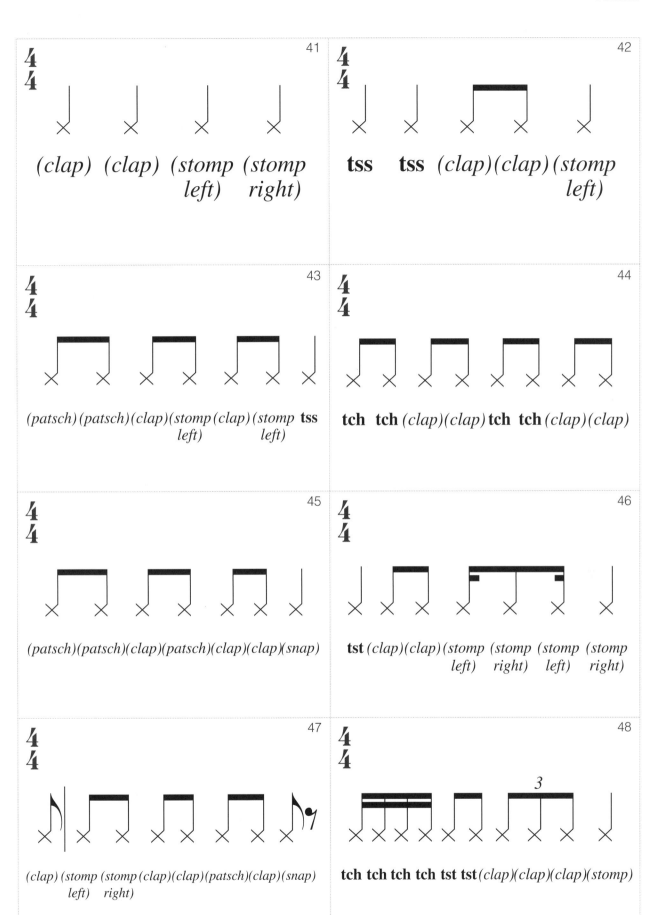

PREPARATION

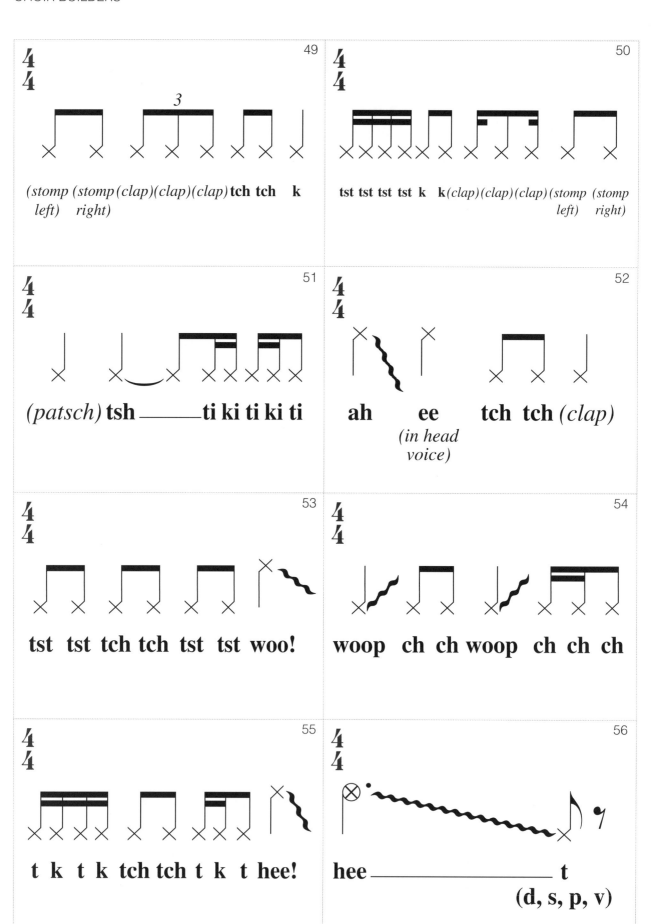

49

4/4

3

(stomp (stomp (clap)(clap)(clap) **tch tch k**
left) right)

50

4/4

tst tst tst tst k k(clap)(clap)(clap)(stomp (stomp
left) right)

51

4/4

(patsch) **tsh ——— ti ki ti ki ti**

52

4/4

ah ee tch tch (clap)
(in head
voice)

53

4/4

tst tst tch tch tst tst woo!

54

4/4

woop ch ch woop ch ch ch

55

4/4

t k t k tch tch t k t hee!

56

4/4

hee ——————— t
(d, s, p, v)

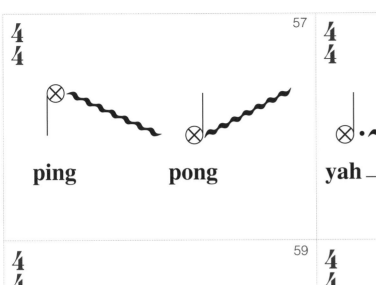

57

ping   **pong**

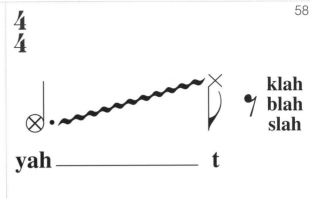

58

klah
blah
slah

yah ———————— **t**

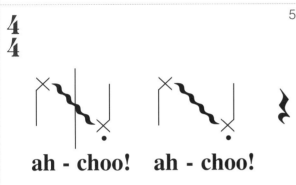

59

ah - choo!   **ah - choo!**

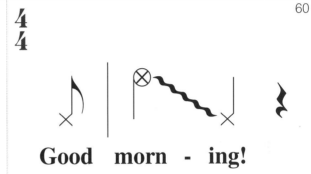

60

Good   **morn - ing!**

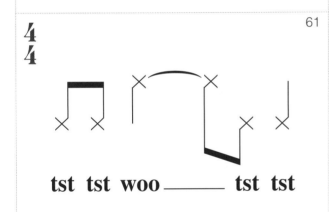

61

tst tst woo ———— **tst tst**

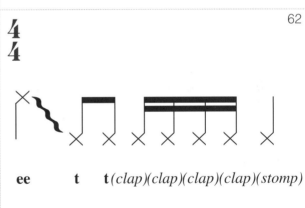

62

ee   **t**   **t** *(clap)(clap)(clap)(clap)(stomp)*

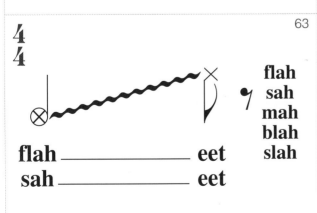

63

flah
sah
mah
blah
slah

flah ———— **eet**
sah ———— **eet**

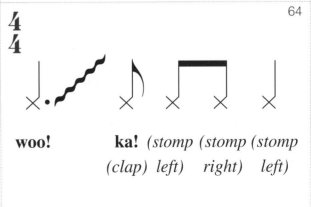

64

woo!   **ka!** *(stomp (stomp (stomp*
(clap) left) right) left)

PREPARATION

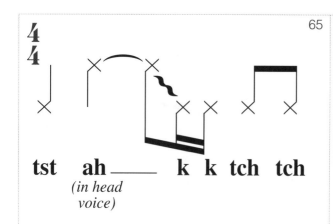

tst ah ____ k k tch tch
(in head voice)

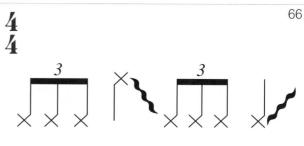

tch tch tch ping! tch tch tch pong!

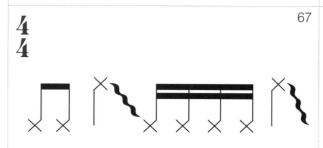

tch tch whoo! *(clap)(clap)(clap)(clap)* **hee!**

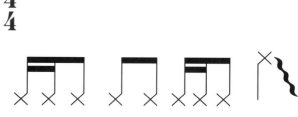

tch tch tch *(clap)(clap)* **tst tst tst woo!**

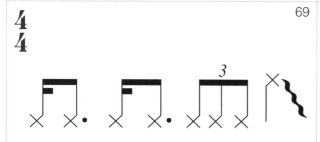

(clap)(clap)(snap (snap **tch tch tch woo!**
          L)   R)

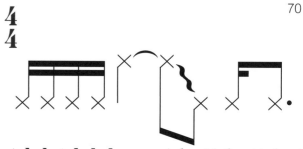

tch k tch k hee ___*(clap)(clap)(clap)*
(head voice)

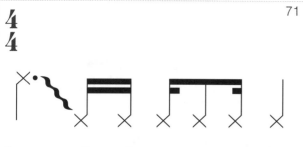

hee tch tch tst tst tst cha

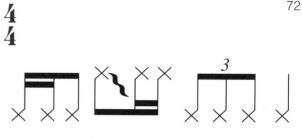

ch ch k who ti ki ch ch ch kah
(siren)

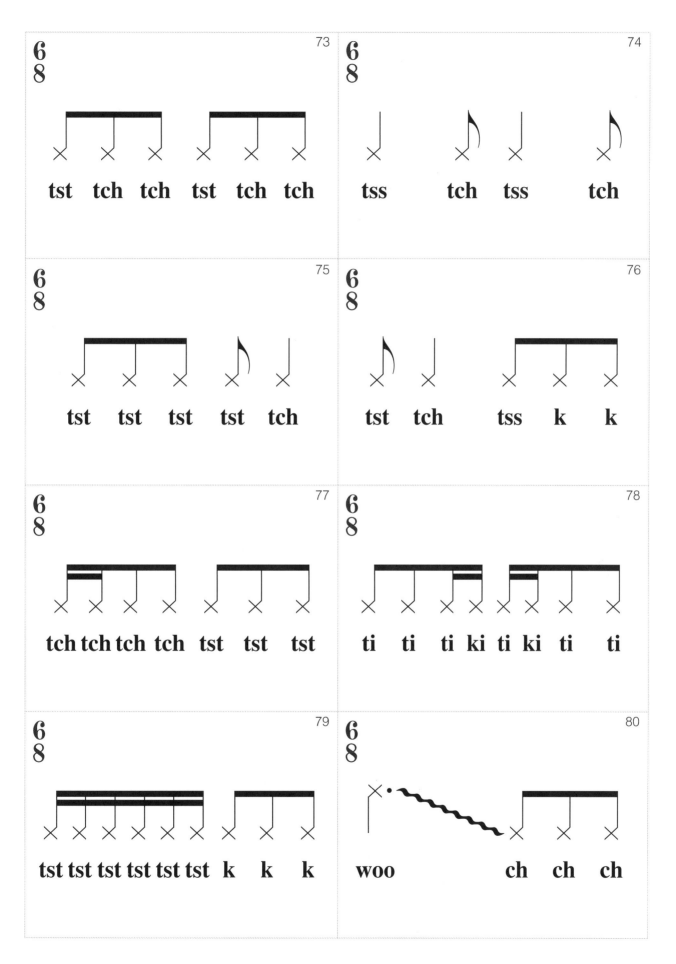

PREPARATION

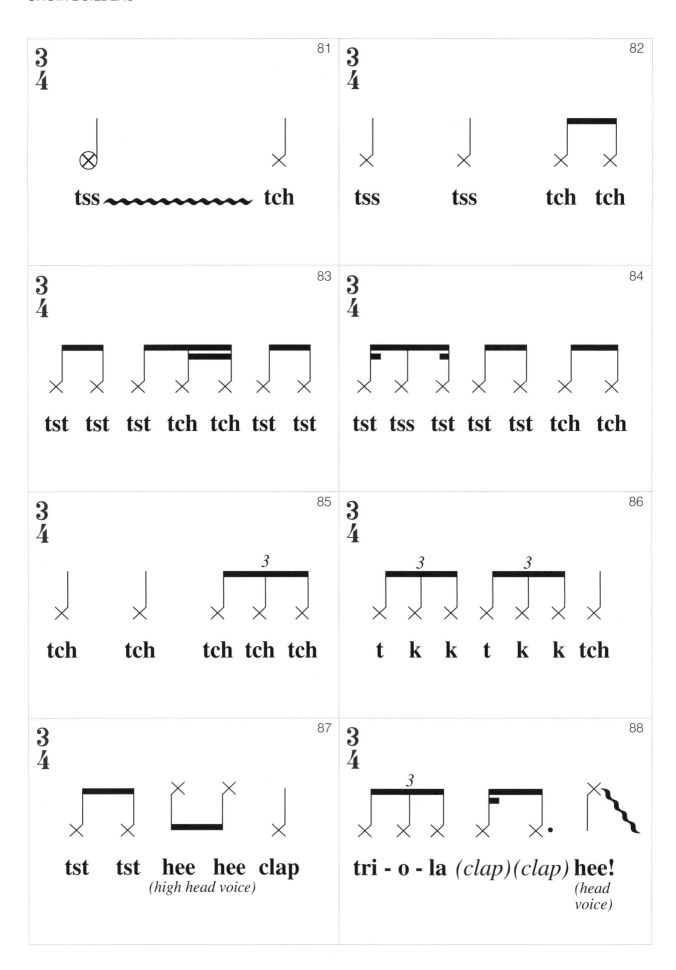

81

$\frac{3}{4}$

tss ～～～～～～～ tch

82

$\frac{3}{4}$

tss   tss   tch   tch

83

$\frac{3}{4}$

tst tst tst tch tch tst tst

84

$\frac{3}{4}$

tst tss tst tst tst tch tch

85

$\frac{3}{4}$

tch   tch   tch tch tch

86

$\frac{3}{4}$

t   k   k   t   k   k   tch

87

$\frac{3}{4}$

tst   tst   hee   hee   clap

(high head voice)

88

$\frac{3}{4}$

tri - o - la *(clap)(clap)* **hee!**

(head voice)

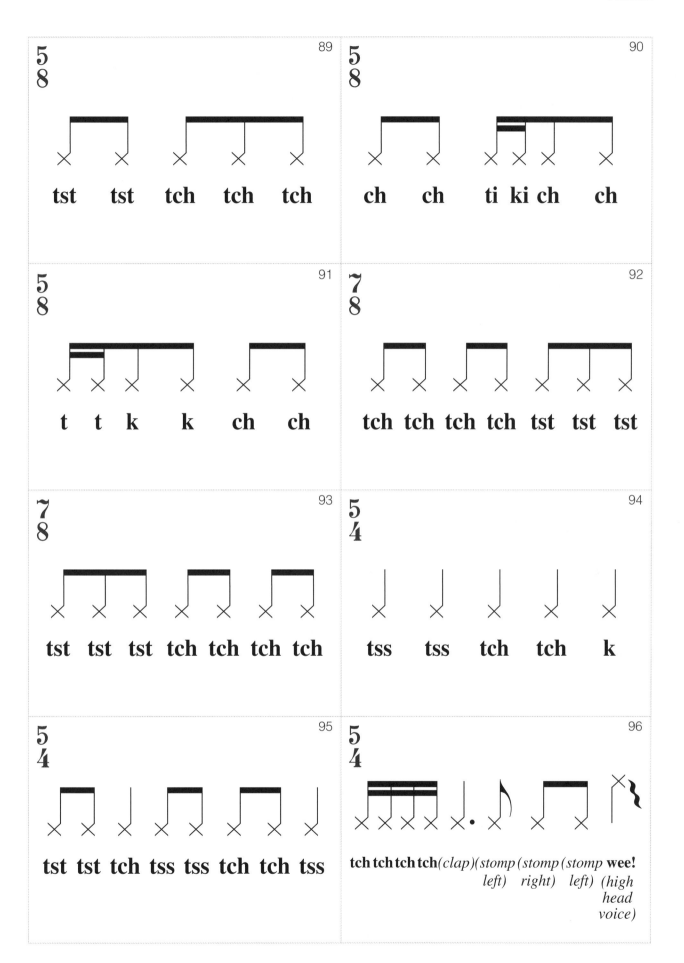

UNISON

MAY WE FOLLOW YOU?

Page 50

FOCAL POINTS

- activating head voice
- intonation (descending line)
- tall vowels

EXPLANATION

- Sing this exercise with a well supported singing tone (in head voice).
- Carefully use your ear to keep each pitch in tune.
- Employ nice, tall vowel sounds throughout the exercise.

EXPANSION

- Vary the dynamics (pp, p, mp, mf, f, ff, crescendo, decrescendo).
- Vary the articulations (staccato, legato, tenuto, accent, marcato).
- Use Multiple Expression Levels (M.E.L.)

EXTENSION

- Use solfege syllables.
- As you sing the exercise, extend your right arm outward in an inviting manner.

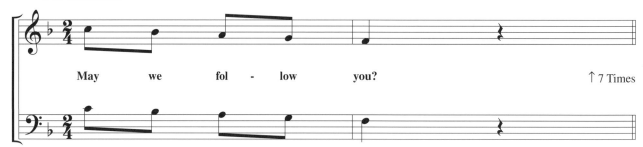

May   we   fol - low   you?   ↑ 7 Times

WEE OH WEE!

Page 51

FOCAL POINTS

- maintaining head voice
- descending intervals

EXPLANATION

- Sing the exercise using all head voice tones.
- Keep all of the pitches in tune as you sing.

EXPANSION

- Vary the vowel sounds.

EXTENSION

- Sing this piece expressively using a sweeping motion with your hand (as if you are painting a wall).

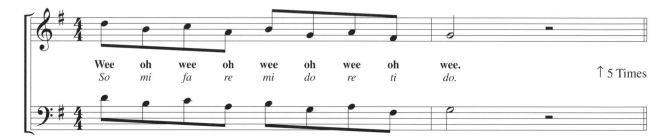

Wee   oh   wee   oh   wee   oh   wee   oh   wee.
So   mi   fa   re   mi   do   re   ti   do.   ↑ 5 Times

4   AH! PHRASE (DESCENDING)

Page 52

FOCAL POINTS

- intonation
- phrasing

EXPLANATION

- Sing this phrase carefully, paying close attention to intonation. Try to sing the entire phrase without taking a breath.

EXPANSION

- Vary the vowel sounds (ee, oh, oo).
- Vary the dynamics (pp, p, mp, mf, f, ff, crescendo, decrescendo).
- Vary the articulations (staccato, legato, tenuto, accent, marcato).
- Use Multiple Expression Levels (M.E.L.)

EXTENSION

- Use solfege syllables.

Ah.   ↑ 5 Times

UNISON

5   SYNCOPATION SOUND

Page 53

FOCAL POINTS

- syncopation (rhythm)
- intonation (descending half steps)

EXPLANATION

- Sing this exercise with rhythmic accuracy. Be sure to maintain a relaxed rhythmic feel. Keep your eyebrows lifted as you sing the descending line.

EXPANSION

- Sing each syllable of the word "syn-co-pa-tion" in a staccato style; crescendo on the word "sound."

EXTENSION

- For each phrase, use the following movement: patsch, patsch, clap, clap, snap.
- Create alternate movement for this exercise.

Syn - co - pa - tion   sound! _____   Syn - co - pa - tion   sound! _

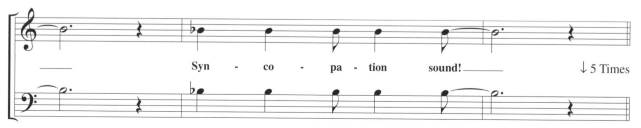

_____   Syn - co - pa - tion   sound! _____   ↓ 5 Times

UNISON

...AH!

...NTS

- ...f head voice
- ... interval
- ...g scale
- singing with expression

EXPLANATION

- Sing this exercise with clarity of tone, emphasizing the ascending perfect fifth interval. Be sure to energize the first note of the phrase, sing through the high note, then taper the dynamics (get slightly softer) as the phrase comes to a close.

EXPANSION

- Vary the vowel sounds (use ee, oo, oh).
- Use Multiple Expression Levels (M.E.L.)

EXTENSION

- As you sing the perfect fifth interval, simulate various sports activities using your hands and upper body. Use your hands to "follow through" the motions of the sports activity as you conclude the phrase. Sample sports activities include: throwing a basketball (three point shot); throwing a football (a 50-yard pass); batting a baseball; bowling; hitting a golf ball (teeing off); throwing a Frisbee.

Ah

↑ 4 Times

7 HIPPETY HOP!

Page 55

FOCAL POINTS

- articulations (staccato versus tenuto)
- descending thirds
- diction
- raised fourth degree (fi)

EXPLANATION

- Sing this piece with good diction, observing all the articulation markings.
- Sing all the intervals, especially the descending thirds, with good intonation.

EXPANSION

- Vary the text, singing the entire exercise on "tah."

EXTENSION

- Conduct this piece using a two beat pattern. Use short, crisp, down and up gestures to show the staccato style.

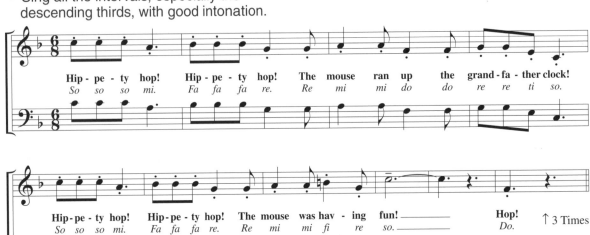

Hip - pe - ty hop! Hip - pe - ty hop! The mouse ran up the grand - fa - ther clock!
So so so mi. Fa fa fa re. Re mi mi do do re re ti so.

Hip - pe - ty hop! Hip - pe - ty hop! The mouse was hav - ing fun! Hop!
So so so mi. Fa fa fa re. Re mi mi fi re so. Do. ↑ 3 Times

8 SPACE TO HOLD A PING-PONG BALL

Page 58

FOCAL POINTS

- interval of a perfect fourth
- maintaining tall vowels
- activating head voice

EXPLANATION

- Sing this exercise carefully, making sure that all pitches are in tune.
- Maintain good head voice, and keep those vowels nice and tall.

EXPANSION

- Vary the dynamics (pp, p, mp, mf, f, ff, crescendo, decrescendo).
- Vary the articulations (staccato, legato, tenuto, accent, marcato).
- Use Multiple Expression Levels (M.E.L.)

EXTENSION

- Using a random pitch given by the teacher, sing this exercise.

UNISON

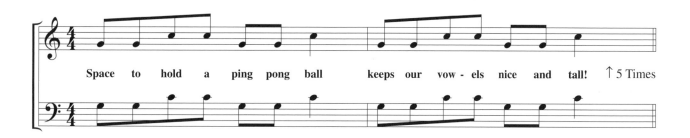

9 TWO TIGERS TANGO

Page 60

FOCAL POINTS

- diction
- minor mode
- phrasing

EXPLANATION

- Sing this pattern with clarity of diction and pitch, all in one breath.

EXPANSION

- Vary the dynamics (pp, p, mp, mf, f, ff, crescendo, decrescendo)
- Vary the articulations (staccato, legato, tenuto, accent, marcato)
- Multiple Expression Levels (M.E.L.)

EXTENSION

- Use solfege syllables.
- Research the tango dance style and discuss its history with the class. (MENC Standard #9).

10 FALLING SNOWFLAKES

Page 62

FOCAL POINTS

- diction
- intonation

EXPLANATION

- Sing the exercise with crisp, clean consonants.

EXPANSION

- Vary the dynamics (pp, p, mp, mf, f, ff, crescendo, decrescendo).
- Vary the articulations (staccato, legato, tenuto, accent, marcato).
- Use Multiple Expression Levels (M.E.L.)

EXTENSION

- Use solfege syllables.
- Conduct this piece using a two-pattern ("down-up" motion) as you sing.

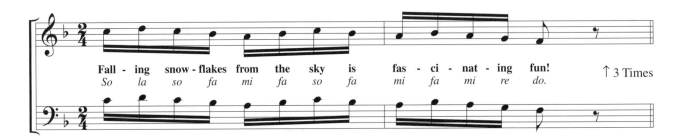

11 HOW WIDE THE SKY

Page 63

FOCAL POINTS

- intonation
- arpeggios
- diction
- expression
- diphthongs

EXPLANATION

- Sing the exercise using tall vowels. For each diphthong (how, wide, sky), Sustain the first vowel sound as long as possible. The second vowel sound should be sung as quickly as possible, just at the point of completing the word.

EXPANSION

- Vary the dynamics (pp, p, mp, mf, f, ff, crescendo, decrescendo).
- Vary the articulations (staccato, legato, tenuto, accent, marcato).
- Use Multiple Expression Levels (M.E.L.)
- Use solfege syllables for this exercise.

EXTENSION

- As you sing the word "wide," extend your hands upward and outward to accompany the phrase.

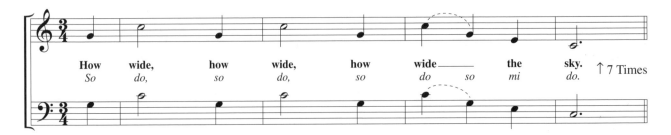

18

12 MOVING OVER MOUNTAINS

Page 66

FOCAL POINTS

- rhythmic accuracy
- natural minor scale

EXPLANATION

- Sing this piece with both rhythmic and tonal accuracy.

EXPANSION

- Vary the dynamics (pp, p, mp, mf, f, ff, crescendo, decrescendo).
- Vary the articulations (staccato, legato, tenuto, accent, marcato).
- Use Multiple Expression Levels (M.E.L.)

EXTENSION

- Chant the rhythms of this piece using the Kodály rhythm syllables.
- Using percussion instruments and or body percussion, compose a rhythmic ostinato to accompany this pattern (MENC Standards #2, 4).

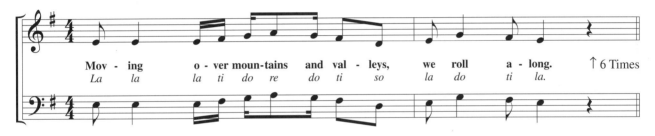

Moving o - ver moun-tains and val - leys, we roll a - long.   ↑ 6 Times
La   la   la ti do re   do ti   so   la do   ti la.

13 HOW DO YOU DO?

Page 68

FOCAL POINTS

- singing with expression
- breath control
- pentatonic scale

EXPLANATION

- Sing each short phrase using good vocal and facial expression. Identify which pitches of the traditional diatonic scale are not present.

EXPANSION

- Place a staccato marking on the word "how" and a tenuto marking on the word "do" that immediately follows.
- Allow each phrase to build in dynamic level and in intensity. Allow the last phrase to get softer.

EXTENSION

- March around the room, greeting your neighbor as your sing this piece. Be sure to maintain a steady tempo as you move about the room.

How do you do? How do you do? How do you do? How do you do to - day? _____   ↑ 5 Times
So   do re do. So   do re do. So   do re mi re   do la so la do. _____

UNISON

14 THE MINOR THIRD

Page 71

FOCAL POINTS

- the minor third interval
- syncopation

EXPLANATION

- Sing the minor third intervals with accuracy.
- Sing the syncopated rhythms with clarity and in a relaxed manner.

EXPANSION

- Use only staccato articulations throughout the piece.

EXTENSION

- Create your own scat syllables (such as doo, bah, bop) and sing this exercise.
- Once you become familiar with the melody, try to improvise your own new tune (MENC Standard #3).
- While keeping the melody of this exercise in mind, try to sing a minor third interval from random pitches given by the teacher.

UNISON

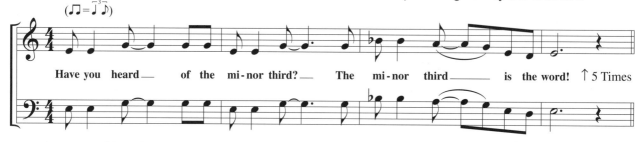

15 AH! PHRASE (ASCENDING)

Page 74

FOCAL POINTS

- singing arpeggios in tune
- singing with expression
- tonic versus subdominant harmony

EXPLANATION

- Sing this piece using good intonation and expression. Listen as you sing to hear the two different harmonic progressions.

EXPANSION

- Vary the vowel sounds (ee, oh, oo).
- Add consonants to the beginnings of the vowel sounds (for example, too, kee, poh).

EXTENSION

- Add solfege syllables to this piece as a way of further understanding the components of the arpeggios performed.
- Given a single pitch by the teacher, try to sing the tonic and subdominant arpeggios from that pitch.

16 GO TEAM, GO!

Page 76

FOCAL POINTS

- intonation (leading tone)
- diction
- steady beat

EXPLANATION

- Sing this exercise with crisp, clean consonants. Be sure to keep all pitches in tune, especially the leading tone (ti).
- Maintain a steady beat throughout the exercise.

EXPANSION

- Vary the dynamics (pp, p, mp, mf, f, ff, crescendo, decrescendo).
- Vary the articulations (staccato, legato, tenuto, accent, marcato).
- Use Multiple Expression Levels (M.E.L.)

EXTENSION

- As you vary the articulations, create appropriate movement (using only your hands and arms) to accompany your performance.

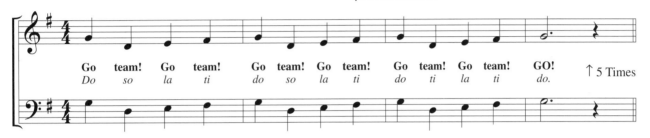

Go team! Go team! Go team! Go team! Go team! Go team! GO!   ↑ 5 Times
Do so la ti do so la ti do ti la ti do.

UNISON

17 CANTANTE CON EXPRESIÓN

Page 78

FOCAL POINTS

- singing with expression
- dotted eighth-sixteenth rhythm
- tonic, subdominant and dominant harmonies

EXPLANATION

- Sing this piece with appropriate vocal and facial expression.
- Sing all the rhythmic patterns, especially the dotted-eighth and sixteenth combinations, with accuracy.

- Sing all the intervals and resulting harmonies with accurate intonation.

EXPANSION

- Use solfege syllables.

EXTENSION

- Using percussion instruments and/or body percussion (patsch, clap, snap, stomp), create an ostinato to accompany this exercise. Notate your ostinato pattern (MENC Standards #2, 4 and 5).

Oh! _____ Can - tan - te con ex - pre - sión. Can - tan - te con ex -
So! _____ Do do do mi mi so mi. Mi fa fa la la

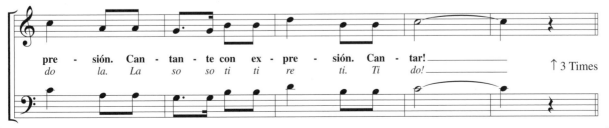

pre - sión. Can - tan - te con ex - pre - sión. Can - tar! _____   ↑ 3 Times
do la. La so so ti ti re ti. Ti do! _____

21

18 LONG PHRASES

Page 81

FOCAL POINTS

• singing intervals in tune
• breath control

EXPLANATION

• Sing each phrase with energy and pitch accuracy.
• Take a good breath as you prepare to sing each phrase.

EXPANSION

• Vary the dynamics (pp, p, mp, mf, f, ff, crescendo, decrescendo).
• Vary the articulations (staccato, legato, tenuto, accent, marcato).
• Use Multiple Expression Levels (M.E.L.)

EXTENSION

• Sing this exercise using numbers.
• Sing this exercise using moveable do, along with the Kodály hand signs.

UNISON

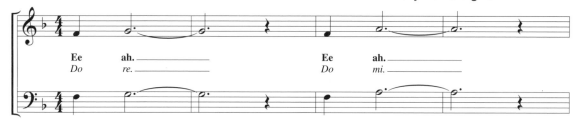

19 TELL ME WHAT YOU KNOW

Page 85

FOCAL POINTS

• diction
• major scale
• lowered seventh degree (te)

EXPLANATION

• As you sing this piece, be sure to enunciate all words clearly.
• Keep the scale tones in tune as you sing (ascending and descending).
• Observe the lowered seventh scale degree (te).

EXPANSION

• Vary the dynamics (pp, p, mp, mf, f, ff, crescendo, decrescendo).
• Vary the articulations (staccato, legato, tenuto, accent, marcato).
• Use Multiple Expression Levels (M.E.L.)

EXTENSION

• Select a small group of singers to sing and sustain the tonic pitch (as a descant) while the rest of the class sings the exercise. Use a neutral syllable (ah or ooh).

20 I WILL SING THIS SONG FOR YOU

Page 87

FOCAL POINTS

- major third versus minor third (mi, me)
- syncopation

EXPLANATION

- Sing this blues-style piece, carefully distinguishing between the major and minor scale patterns.
- Perform the syncopated patterns with rhythmic ease and clarity.

EXPANSION

- Vary the dynamics from phrase to phrase.
- Multiple Expression Levels (M.E.L.)

EXTENSION

- Sing this piece using scat syllables of your choice (doo, bee, dah, bah, etc.) (MENC Standard #3).

UNISON

21 DICTION UNDERSTOOD?

Page 90

UNISON

FOCAL POINTS

- diction
- diatonic scale

EXPLANATION

- Sing this piece with good diction (crisp, clean consonants).
- Pay close attention to all intervals as you sing.

EXPANSION

- Vary the dynamics (pp, p, mp, mf, f, ff, crescendo, decrescendo).
- Vary the articulations (staccato, legato, tenuto, accent, marcato).
- Use Multiple Expression Levels (M.E.L.)

EXTENSION

- Use solfege syllables.
- Using all quarter note durations, perform the following "bass" line to accompany this piece: do, do, do, do, so, so, so, do.

If I want my dic - tion to be clear and un - der - stood.
Do ti do re mi re mi fa so fa so do so.

Lips and teeth and tip of tongue will help it to be good.
Fa mi re fa mi re do mi re do ti re do.

↑ 3 Times

UNISON (OPT. 2-PART)

22 SOAP OPERA

Page 92

FOCAL POINTS
- singing with expression
- intervals (major second versus minor second)

EXPLANATION
- Perform this piece with lots of expression, pretending that you are providing background music for a dramatic soap opera.

EXPANSION
- Vary the vowel sound (ee, oh).
- Vary the articulations.
- Use Multiple Expression Levels (M.E.L.)

EXTENSION
- As you sing the exercise, pantomime the activity of playing a string instrument (violin, viola or cello). Discuss how this activity can help you sing with more expression.
- Once you understand the chord progression of this piece, improvise your own melody (MENC Standard #3).

23 UP ABOVE THE TREE

Page 94

FOCAL POINTS
- diction
- head voice
- descending major scale
- singing with expression

EXPLANATION
- Sing this piece expressively, floating in head voice on the high note.
- Keep the piece in tune as you sing a descending major scale.
- Use good diction.

EXPANSION
- Vary the dynamics (pp, p, mp, mf, f, ff, crescendo, decrescendo).
- Vary the articulations (staccato, legato, tenuto, accent, marcato).
- Vary the vowel sounds (ee, ooh, ah).
- Use Multiple Expression Levels (M.E.L.)

EXTENSION
- Use the Kodály hand signs as you sing. Be expressive!

SODA POP CANS (2-Part Treble)

24

Page 96

FOCAL POINTS

- intervals in the tonic triad
- two-part harmony
- use of head voice
- singing with expression
- clarity of diction

EXPLANATION

- Use this piece as a way to secure intonation, develop stability in singing two-part harmony, and develop expression as you communicate the text.
- Singers on the top vocal part should work to float and sustain the "ah" vowel.
- Make sure that every word can be understood.

EXPANSION

- Whisper the text in rhythm at a pianissimo dynamic level. Over-enunciate the diction to ensure that all consonants are clean.

EXTENSION

- Without the accompaniment CD, try singing each successive verse at a slightly faster tempo.
- Using your entire body, act out the lyrics as you sing.

UNISON (OPT. 2-PART)

25

ALL OVER TOWN

Page 102

FOCAL POINTS

- singing with expression
- syllabic stress
- call and response

EXPLANATION

- Sing this piece expressively.
- Be sure to perform with the appropriate syllabic stress.

EXPANSION

- Vary the dynamics in the call and response (echo) section. The echo should be sung at a softer dynamic level.

EXTENSION

- On the fourth verse, which involves dancing, follow the movements of the teacher (leader).
- Think of additional verses for this piece. Perform as a class (MENC Standard #4).

*improvise dance moves for 4 beats

26

FEEL THE SUBDIVISION

Page 105

FOCAL POINTS

- rhythmic precision
- intonation (ascending scale)

EXPLANATION

- Feel the eighth note pulsation as you sing this piece.
- Sing all intervals with accuracy.

EXPANSION

- Vary the dynamics (pp, p, mp, mf, f, ff, crescendo, decrescendo).
- Vary the articulations (staccato, legato, tenuto, accent, marcato).
- Use Multiple Expression Levels (M.E.L.)

EXTENSION

- Tap the eighth note pulse as you sing the exercise.
- Use a number system to sing this piece.

UNISON (OPT. 2-PART)

27 CORRAL THE CHORALE

FOCAL POINTS

Page 106

- diction
- intonation

EXPLANATION

- Sing this piece using good diction and intonation.

EXPANSION

- Vary the dynamics (pp, p, mp, mf, f, ff, crescendo, decrescendo).
- Vary the articulations (staccato, legato, tenuto, accent, marcato).
- Use Multiple Expression Levels (M.E.L.)

EXTENSION

- Using Orff keyboard instruments, create an orchestration of this work. Some instruments can play melody; some can play the bass line (MENC Standards #2 and 5).

UNISON (OPT. 2-PART)

28

28 TOO-RE-LOO-RE-LOO

Page 108

FOCAL POINTS

• natural minor scale
• intervals (seconds and thirds)

EXPLANATION

• Sing the following exercise in tune, utilizing the natural minor scale mode.

EXPANSION

• Vary the dynamics (pp, p, mp, mf, f, ff, crescendo, decrescendo).
• Vary the articulations (staccato, legato, tenuto, accent, marcato).
• Use Multiple Expression Levels (M.E.L.)

EXTENSION

• Discuss the differences between the natural minor scale and the harmonic minor scale. Employ the harmonic minor scale degree of a raised seventh to this piece. Listen to the differences between the scale patterns and discuss them (MENC Standards #4 and 6).

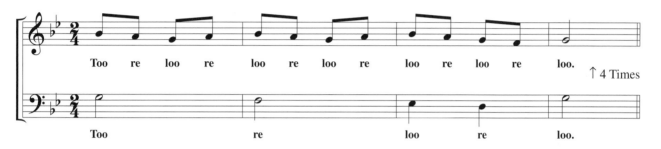

Too   re   loo   re   loo   re   loo   re   loo   re   loo   re   loo.

↑ 4 Times

Too   re   loo   re   loo.

UNISON (OPT. 2-PART)

Page 109

29 TAKIN' A TRIP AROUND THE WORLD

FOCAL POINTS

- natural minor scale
- diction
- expression

EXPLANATION

- Sing this piece in tune, paying close attention to the elements that make up the natural minor scale.
- Maintain crisp consonants and tall vowels.
- Use the appropriate vocal and facial expressions while singing the piece.

EXPANSION

- Use a neutral syllable (such as "doo").
- Use Multiple Expression Levels (M.E.L.)

EXTENSION

- Think of other cities and countries that you would like to highlight. Consult with your geography teacher to find out other places of interest. Play games to see if you can identify other places as you sing the song (MENC Standard #8 and 9).
- In measures 9-12 of this exercise, change the action verb from "flying" to "sailing," "driving," or other relevant words (MENC Standard #4).

*Argentina or your choice

UNISON (OPT. 2-PART)

MINER FORTY-NINER

Page 111

FOCAL POINTS

- intonation
- diction
- melodic minor scale

EXPLANATION

- Sing this piece with good diction.
- Carefully pay attention to the intonation as you sing, maintaining awareness of the elements in the melodic minor scale.

EXPANSION

- Sing this piece as a round (begin the round after one full measure).

EXTENSION

- Research the California gold rush of 1849. Share your findings with your music and/or social studies class (MENC Standard #9).

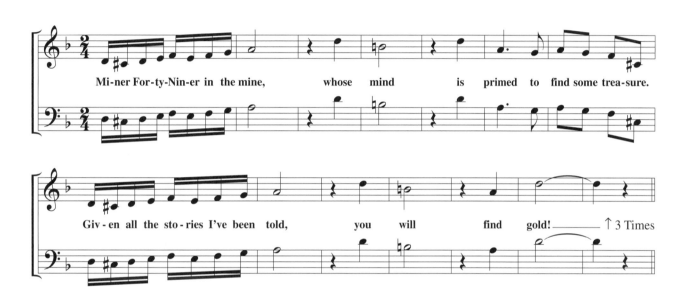

Mi-ner For-ty-Nin-er in the mine, whose mind is primed to find some trea-sure.

Giv-en all the sto-ries I've been told, you will find gold! ↑ 3 Times

UNISON (OPT. 2-PART)

2-PART TREBLE OR MIXED

31 MAY WE FOLLOW YOU? (2-PART)

Page 114

FOCAL POINTS

- ascending scale
- singing with expression

EXPLANATION

- Sing the piece with an lively and expressive tone.
- Be aware of the intervals involved as you sing the ascending and descending scale tones.

EXPANSION

- Vary the dynamics (pp, p, mp, mf, f, ff, crescendo, decrescendo).
- Vary the articulations (staccato, legato, tenuto, accent, marcato).
- Use Multiple Expression Levels (M.E.L.)

EXTENSION

- As you vary the articulations, also think of varying the mood and character of the piece.
- Think of adjectives to describe various moods, then conduct the piece (using a four pattern). Compare and contrast the feelings that you have when you conduct the various styles.

May we fol - low—— you?
Do do do re mi fa so.

May we fol - low—— you?
So so so fa mi re do.

↑ 4 Times

May we fol - low you?
Do do so do mi.

32

RING DEM BELLS

Page 116

FOCAL POINTS

- intonation (descending fourths)
- articulations (marcato-staccato)
- lowered seventh degree (te)

EXPLANATION

- As you sing this exercise, try to perform the descending fourth intervals with accuracy.
- Carefully observe the articulation markings.

EXPANSION

- Vary the dynamics (pp, p, mp, mf, f, ff, crescendo, decrescendo).
- Vary the articulations (staccato, legato, tenuto, accent, marcato).
- Use Multiple Expression Levels (M.E.L.)

EXTENSION

- Simulate the "bell ringing" motion by conducting a four pattern (down, in, out, up) as you walk around the room (to a quarter note pulse) and sing.

33

THE GROWING PHRASE

Page 118

FOCAL POINTS

- singing with expression
- singing repetitive pitches
- descending major scale (so, fa, mi, re, do)

EXPLANATION

- Use this exercise as an opportunity to keep repetitive pitches in tune.
- Focus on using good intonation as you sing the descending scale.

EXPANSION

- Vary the dynamics (pp, p, mp, mf, f, ff, crescendo, decrescendo).
- Vary the articulations (staccato, legato, tenuto, accent, marcato).
- Use Multiple Expression Levels (M.E.L.)

EXTENSION

- As the phrase continues to expand, discuss and develop some appropriate gestures to illustrate this concept.

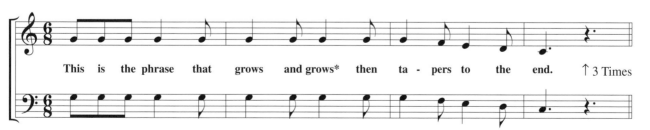

*Add one more "and grows" each time

2-PART TREBLE OR MIXED

Page 120

34 INTERVALLIC EXPANSION

FOCAL POINTS

- intonation
- internalization of intervals (fourths, fifths, sixths, sevenths, octaves)

EXPLANATION

- As you sing through the exercise, use extra care to sing all of the intervals with precision and accuracy. Try to visualize and internally hear the intervals before and as you sing them.

EXPANSION

- Use numbers and solfege syllables to assist you in this exercise.

EXTENSION

- When you are not using the accompaniment track, practice "freezing" each interval as you sing it. Close your eyes and concentrate on the distance between the pitches in each interval.

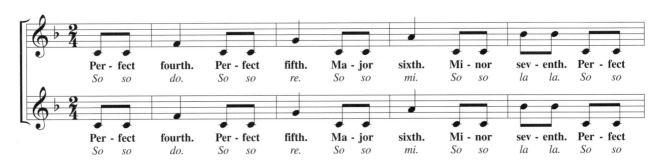

↑ 3 Times

2-PART TREBLE OR MIXED

35

TRIPLETS

Page 123

FOCAL POINTS

- rhythmic accuracy

EXPLANATION

- Use this exercise to experience the triplet feel.

EXPANSION

- Vary the dynamics.
- Change the syllable to "la," "ta," "fa" and "ka" to develop clarity of consonants.

EXTENSION

- Sing the piece several times, placing an accent on a different note within the triplet grouping each time.
- Sing the solfege syllables for Part 2; Part 1 is written for you.

36

TWO NOTE PHRASES (SIXTHS)

Page 125

FOCAL POINTS

- intervals (sixths)
- two-part harmony
- phrasing

EXPLANATION

- Sing each two-note phrase expressively, giving emphasis to the first note of each grouping.
- Listen as you sing, carefully holding on to your vocal part.

EXPANSION

- Vary the vowel sound.
- Vary the articulations (accent on the first note, staccato on the second).

EXTENSION

- Create a gentle, "down-up" motion with your hands to accompany the two-note phrase patterns.
- Sing the solfege syllables for Part 2; Part 1 is written for you.

2-PART TREBLE OR MIXED

37 TWO NOTE PHRASES (TENTHS)

Page 128

FOCAL POINTS

- intervals (tenths)
- two-part harmony
- phrasing

EXPLANATION

- Sing each two-note phrase expressively, giving emphasis to the first note of each grouping.
- Listen as you sing, carefully holding on to your vocal part.

EXPANSION

- Vary the vowel sound.
- Vary the articulations (accent on the first note, staccato on the second).

EXTENSION

- Create a gentle, "down-up" motion with your hands to accompany the two-note phrase patterns.
- Sing the solfege syllables for Part 2; Part 1 is written for you.

Tah, tah, tah, tah, tah tah tah.
Mi fa fa so so la ti do ti do re do.

Tah, tah, tah, tah, tah tah tah.
Do ti ti la la so la(fa) so(mi) fa(re) mi(do) re(ti) do.

↑ 3 Times

38 STAGGER YOUR BREATHING

Page 131

FOCAL POINTS

- breath control
- harmonic minor mode

EXPLANATION

- Sing this piece using good breath support and breath control.
- Use your ear to secure accurate intonation in the harmonic mode.

EXPANSION

- Vary the vowel sound.
- Use accents on each note.

EXTENSION

- Conduct this piece as you sing it.
- Create an "arch" motion with your arm as you sing through the phrase.

Ooh. ↑ 3 Times

2-PART TREBLE OR MIXED

39 WILLOW TREE

Page 133

FOCAL POINTS
- major versus minor scale patterns
- tonic versus subdominant harmony

EXPLANATION
- Sing this exercise carefully, paying close attention to the major and minor intervals involved.
- Try to distinguish the change in harmony. (from tonic to subdominant)

EXPANSION
- Vary the articulations (accent, tenuto, staccato, legato).
- Use Multiple Expression Levels (M.E.L.)

EXTENSION
- What other kinds of tree names can you insert into the lyrics of this piece? Consult with a science teacher and do some research on other tree types (MENC Standard #8).

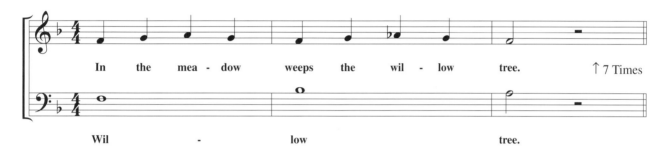

40 CANOE SONG

Page 135

FOCAL POINTS
- diction
- intonation in the minor mode
- syncopation

EXPLANATION
- Sing this exercise with clarity of diction, intonation, and rhythm.

EXPANSION
- Vary the articulations (accent, tenuto, staccato, legato).
- Use Multiple Expression Levels (M.E.L.)

EXTENSION
- Sing this piece using Kodaly rhythm syllables.
- Using percussion instruments, improvise an accompaniment for this piece (MENC Standard #3).

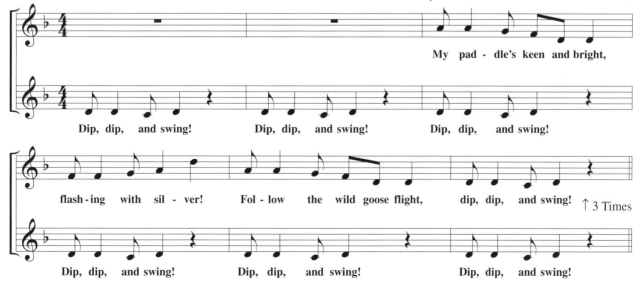

2-PART TREBLE OR MIXED

41 OH SHENANDOAH

Page 138

FOCAL POINTS

• Singing in two-part harmony

EXPLANATION

• Practice singing your part against the other part. When you are secure on your part, switch to learn and master the other part.

EXPANSION

• Add a slight crescendo to notes that are to be sustained.

EXTENSION

• Do some research on this piece. Where does it come from? What does it refer to? (MENC Standard #9).

42 SOON I WILL BE DONE

Page 139

FOCAL POINTS

• intonation (melodic minor mode)
• diction
• breath control

EXPLANATION

• Sing this piece with clarity of diction, making sure that all consonants are clear.

• Read the score carefully as you sing, paying close attention to the raised 7th as you sing up the scale and the lowered 7th as you sing down the scale.

• Take a good breath to sustain the phrase.

EXPANSION

• Vary the dynamics (pp, p, mp, mf, f, ff, crescendo, decrescendo).

• Vary the articulations (staccato, legato, tenuto, accent, marcato).

• Use Multiple Expression Levels (M.E.L.)

EXTENSION

• This piece is an African American spiritual. Do some research on this piece to find out the significance of the text and its relationship to slavery (MENC Standard #8, 9).

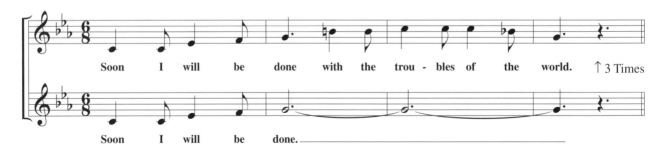

2-PART TREBLE OR MIXED

43 DOO BAH DOO BAH

Page 140

FOCAL POINTS

- syncopation
- vocal jazz stylings

EXPLANATION

- This exercise will assist in making syncopation patterns more smooth and easier to perform.
- Use a light vocal tone to help create the appropriate tone for singing in the jazz style.
- Perform this piece with a swing rhythm.

EXPANSION

- Vary the dynamics (pp, p, mp, mf, f, ff, crescendo, decrescendo).
- Vary the articulations (staccato, legato, tenuto, accent, marcato).
- Use Multiple Expression Levels (M.E.L.)

EXTENSION

- Using finger snaps on beats 2 and 4, accompany your singing.
- As you become comfortable with the piece, develop and use your own scat syllables (MENC Standard #4).

Doo bah. Doo bah. Doo ___ doo doo bah doo bah, ___ doo bah. ↑ 3 Times

2-PART TREBLE OR MIXED

44 I WILL SING THIS SONG FOR YOU (Canon)

Page 141

FOCAL POINTS

- two-part harmony
- major versus minor intervals

EXPLANATION

- Sing this song as a canon to explore the concept of two-part harmony.
- Listen carefully to the difference between the major third and the minor third intervals.

EXPANSION

- Vary the color of your singing tone. Choose a color (red, blue, green, yellow, orange, purple), sing the song, and justify your interpretation.

EXTENSION

- As you sing, walk to the rhythmic values of the piece as given. The "lead" group should set the style and the walking pattern for the group that must follow. The group that follows should follow the exact steps and patterns as the "lead" group.

2-PART TREBLE OR MIXED

3 OR 4-PART MIXED

SCALE INTO HARMONY

Page 143

FOCAL POINTS

- intonation
- four-part harmony

EXPLANATION

- Use this scale to strengthen four-part singing.
- Carefully listen to the singers around you as you perform this exercise.

EXPANSION

- Vary the dynamics.
- Vary the vowel sounds (ee, oo, ah).

EXTENSION

- Sing this exercise unaccompanied.
- Create suspensions in the alto and/or tenor parts by holding out their parts from measure 5 into the downbeat of measure 6 before allowing them to resolve.

Do re me fa so la ti do. _____ ↑ 3 Times

Do re mi fa so la ti do ti la so fa _____ mi. ↑ 3 Times

Do re mi fa so la ti do ti la _____ so. ↑ 3 Times

Do re mi fa so la ti do ti la so fa mi re so do. ↑ 3 Times

46 SCALE WITH PEDAL POINTS

Page 145

FOCAL POINTS

- intonation
- four-part harmony

EXPLANATION

- Use this scale to strengthen four-part singing.
- Carefully listen to the singers around you as you perform this exercise.

EXPANSION

- Vary the dynamics.
- Vary the articulations.

EXTENSION

- Sing this exercise using solfege or numbers.
- Sing this exercise using the Kodály hand signs.
- Re-write this exercise in the parallel harmonic minor mode and perform. Discuss which pitches change and which ones stay the same (MENC Standards #3, 4, 5, 6).

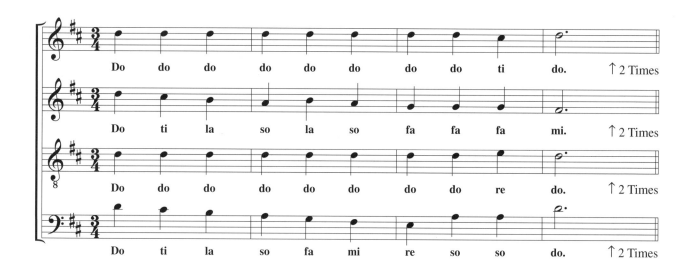

3 OR 4-PART MIXED

47 COMIN' FOR TO CARRY ME HOME

Page 146

FOCAL POINTS

- diction
- syllabic stress
- three-part harmony
- phrasing
- singing with expression

EXPLANATION

- Sing this exercise with clear diction, paying close attention to appropriate syllabic stress.
- Listen carefully as you sing to solidify the three-part harmony.
- Use good breathing technique to sing each phrase expressively.

EXPANSION

- Vary the dynamics.
- Vary the articulations.
- Use Multiple Expression Levels (M.E.L.)

EXTENSION

- The text for this exercise can be found in the African American spiritual "Swing Low, Sweet Chariot." Research this spiritual to uncover the full text of the original spiritual. Discuss how your understanding of this text can effect your performance of the exercise (MENC Standards #6 and 7).

48 ALLELUIA!

Page 148

FOCAL POINTS

- intonation
- four-part harmony
- maintaining tall vowels

EXPLANATION

- Use this scale to strengthen four-part singing.
- Carefully listen to the singers around you as you perform this exercise.
- Be sure to sing tall vowels.

EXPANSION

- Vary the dynamics.
- Vary the articulations.

EXTENSION

- Sing this exercise using solfege or numbers.
- Sing this exercise using the Kodály hand signs.
- Re-write this exercise in the parallel harmonic minor mode and perform. Discuss which pitches change and which ones stay the same (MENC Standards #3, 4, 5, 6).

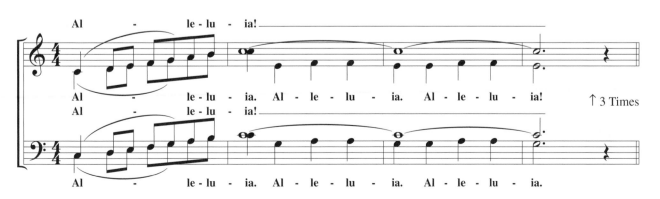

3 OR 4-PART MIXED

49 ROLLING RIVER

Page 150

FOCAL POINTS

- diction
- minor scale (ascending)
- phrasing

EXPLANATION

- Sing this exercise using good diction.
- Be sure to keep the ascending intervals of the minor scale in tune as you sing.
- Use the natural syllabic stress of the words to assist you with phrasing.

EXPANSION

- Vary the dynamics.
- Vary the articulations (staccato, legato, accents, tenuto).

EXTENSION

- In terms of diction, try rolling or flipping the "r's." After listening to this variation in pronunciation, discuss with the ensemble how performance may be affected (MENC Standards #6 and 7).

50

MIDNIGHT INTO MORNING

Page 153

FOCAL POINTS
- singing with expression
- major versus minor mode
- asymmetrical meter (5/4 time)

EXPLANATION
- Sing this piece using appropriate facial and vocal expressions that coincide with the text and the mode.
- Count carefully as you focus on the 5 beat per measure patterns.

EXPANSION
- Vary the dynamics.
- Vary the articulations.
- Use Multiple Expression Levels (M.E.L.)

EXTENSION
- Use solfege syllables to perform this piece.
- Use Kodály hand signs as you sing.
- Learn to conduct in 5/4 meter.

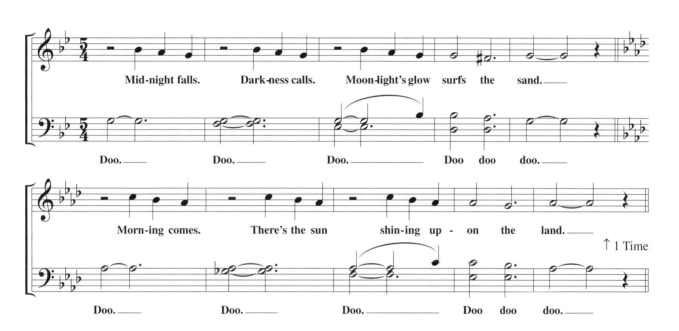

45

51 BEYOND THE SETTING OF THE SUN

Page 155

FOCAL POINTS

- diction
- intervals (intonation)
- phrasing
- anacrusis (as it relates to syllabic stress)

EXPLANATION

- Sing this exercise, paying close attention to clarity of pronunciation and intonation.
- Use the lilting rhythm of the meter to assist you in phrasing and syllabic stress.

EXPANSION

- Vary the dynamics.
- Vary the articulations.
- Use Multiple Expression Levels (M.E.L.)

EXTENSION

- Create new text for this exercise. Use information from another subject area (math, language arts, social studies, or science) as a basis for composing new verses (MENC Standard #4 and 8).

Be - yond the set - ting of the

sun, the night sky flows.＿＿＿ ↑ 2 Times

52 SEVEN SILVER SWANS

Page 156

FOCAL POINTS

- diction
- 6/8 meter
- intonation
- three-part harmony

EXPLANATION

- Use this exercise to build the texture from unison to 2-part, to 3-part.

- Have all singers perform the alto line first. Upon modulating, have the treble voices stay on the alto part, while the male voices switch to their part. With the next modulation, have the sopranos jump to the upper treble part, leaving the altos and baritones on their respective parts.

EXPANSION

- Have the singers "sway" to the dotted-eighth pulse.
- Vary the dynamics.

EXTENSION

- Conduct a two-pattern as you sing the piece.
- Improvise choreography with your arms to show the phrase structure.

↑ 3 Times

3 OR 4-PART MIXED

53 SODA POP CANS (Mixed voices)

Page 159

FOCAL POINTS

- intervals in the tonic triad
- two-part harmony
- use of head voice
- singing with expression
- clarity of diction

EXPLANATION

- Use this piece as a way to secure intonation, develop stability in singing two-part harmony, and develop expression as you communicate the text.
- Singers on the top vocal part should work to float and sustain the "ah" vowel.
- Make sure that every word can be understood.

EXPANSION

- Whisper the text in rhythm at a pianissimo dynamic level. Over-enunciate the diction to ensure that all consonants are clean.

EXTENSION

- Without the accompaniment CD, try singing each successive verse at a slightly faster tempo.
- Using your entire body, act out the lyrics of the score as you sing.
- Determine the corresponding solfege syllables for the first four measures of the piece and use Kodály hand signs while you perform these measures.

↑ 4 Times reducing number of cans each time.

3 OR 4-PART MIXED

48

Page 165

54 GETTING READY TO SING!

FOCAL POINTS

- diction
- syncopated rhythms
- awareness of vocal technique
- artistic expression

EXPLANATION

- Use this warm-up to sequence key choral concepts:

  intake of air
  breath support
  tall vowels
  crisp consonants
  facial expression

EXPANSION

- Vary the tone color.
- Strive for expressive syllabic emphasis on the following syllables:

  READ-y
  Pre-PARE
  Sup-PORT
  VOW-els
  CON-so-nants
  Ex-PRES-sions

EXTENSION

- Use movement suggestions to enhance your performance. Movement found in piano accompaniment.

If we want to be read - y to sing, we must pre - pare the air,* ___ so we can sing ___ our song ___ all day long. ___

↑ 4 Times

*add on each time: "support the sound," "let the vowels be round," "keep the consonants clean," "let our expressions be seen,"

3 OR 4-PART MIXED

2 MAY WE FOLLOW YOU?

Page 14

Voices

May we fol - low   you?   May we fol - low   you?

Piano

May we fol-low   you?   May we fol-low   you?   May we fol-low   you?

May we fol-low   you?   May we fol-low   you?   May we fol-low   you?

WEE OH WEE!

Voices

Wee oh wee oh wee oh wee oh wee.
So mi fa re mi do re ti do.

Wee oh wee oh wee oh wee oh wee.
So mi fa re mi do re ti do.

Piano

Wee oh wee oh wee oh wee oh wee.
So mi fa re mi do re ti do.

Wee oh wee oh wee oh wee oh wee.
So mi fa re mi do re ti do.

Wee oh wee oh wee oh wee oh wee.
So mi fa re mi do re ti do.

Wee oh wee oh wee oh wee oh wee.
So mi fa re mi do re ti do.

UNISON
Piano Accompaniments

4 AH! PHRASE (DESCENDING)

Page 15

Voices

Piano

SYNCOPATION SOUND

SPORTS-AH!

UNISON
Piano Accompaniments

Voices

Piano

Ah _____ Ah _____

Ah _____ Ah _____

Ah _____

7

HIPPETY HOP!

Page 16

Voices
Piano
Hip - pe - ty hop! Hip - pe - ty hop! The mouse ran up the grand-fa - ther clock!
So so so mi. Fa fa fa re. Re mi mi do do re re ti so.
Hip-pe - ty hop! Hip-pe - ty hop! The mouse was hav - ing fun! Hop!
So so so mi. Fa fa fa re. Re mi mi fi re so. Do.
Hip - pe - ty hop! Hip - pe - ty hop! The mouse ran up the grand-fa - ther clock!
So so so mi. Fa fa fa re. Re mi mi do do re re ti so.

UNISON
Piano Accompaniments

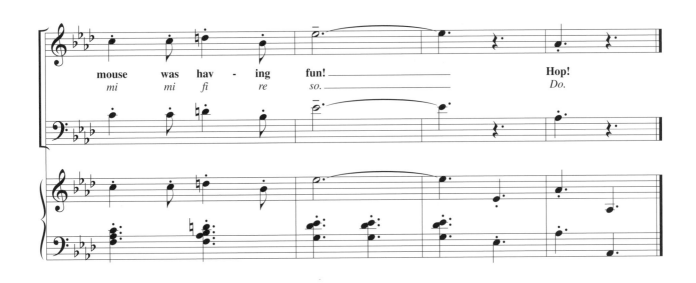

SPACE TO HOLD A PING-PONG BALL

TWO TIGERS TANGO

10 FALLING SNOWFLAKES

Page 18

11 HOW WIDE THE SKY

Page 18

Voices

Piano

UNISON
Piano Accompaniments

12 MOVING OVER MOUNTAINS

Page 19

13 **HOW DO YOU DO?**

Page 19

Voices

Piano

How do you do? How do you do? How do you do? How
So do re do. So do re do. So do re mi re

do you do to - day? _____ How do you do? How
do la so la do. _____ So do re do. So

do you do? How do you do? How do you do to - day? _____ How
do re do. So do re mi re do la so la do. _____ So

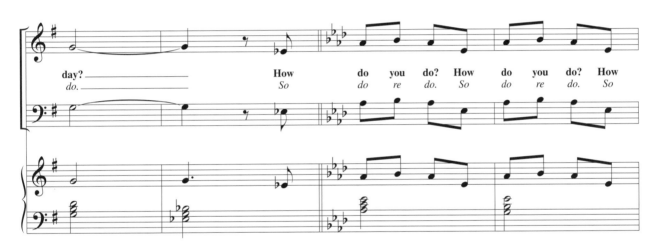

Page 20

14 THE MINOR THIRD

Voices

Piano

Have you heard —— of the mi - nor third? —— The

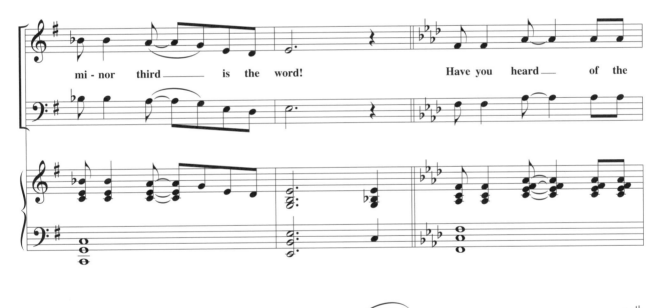

mi - nor third —— is the word! Have you heard —— of the

mi - nor third? —— The mi - nor third —— is the word!

15 AH! PHRASE (ASCENDING)

Page 20

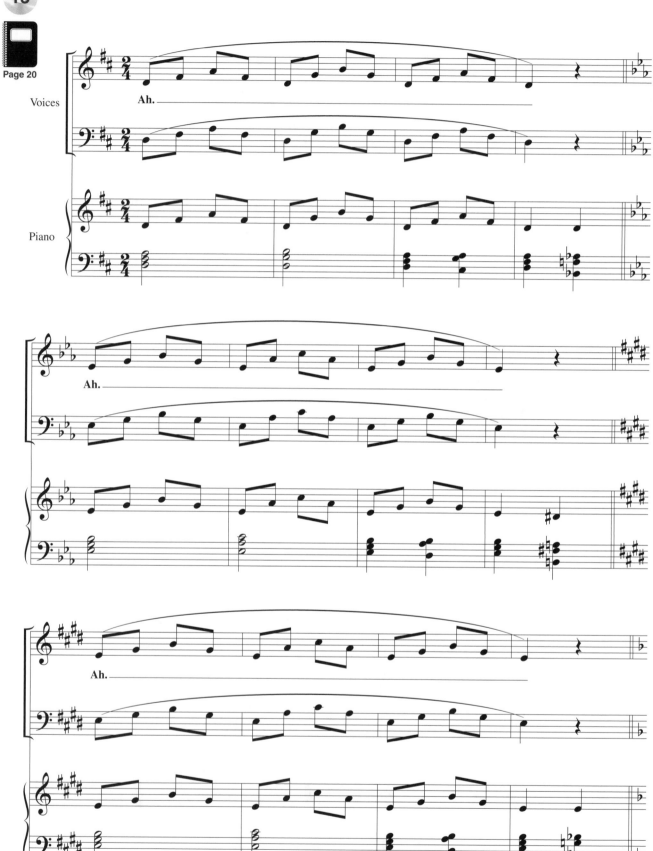

Voices

Ah.

Piano

Ah.

Ah.

16 GO TEAM, GO!

Page 21

UNISON
Piano Accompaniments

Voices

Go team! Go team! Go team! Go team! Go team! Go team! GO!
Do so la ti do so la ti do ti la ti do.

Piano

Go team! Go team! Go team! Go team! Go team! Go team! GO!
Do so la ti do so la ti do ti la ti do.

Go team! Go team! Go team! Go team! Go team! Go team! GO!
Do so la ti do so la ti do ti la ti do.

17 CANTANTE CON EXPRESIÓN

UNISON
Piano Accompaniments

18 LONG PHRASES

Page 22

Voices

Piano

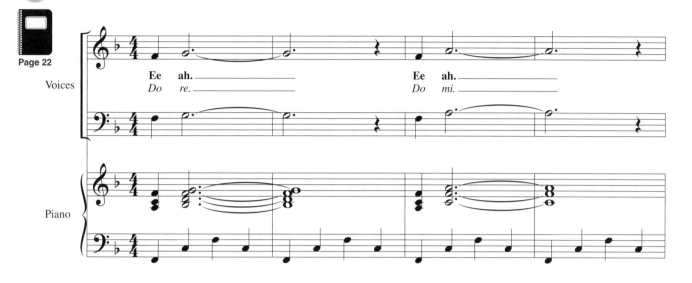

UNISON
Piano Accompaniments

19 TELL ME WHAT YOU KNOW

20 I WILL SING THIS SONG FOR YOU

Page 23

UNISON
Piano Accompaniments

21 DICTION UNDERSTOOD?

Page 24

UNISON
Piano Accompaniments

22 SOAP OPERA

Page 25

Pretend to play string instrument.

UNISON (OPT. 2-PART)
Piano Accompaniments

23 UP ABOVE THE TREE

Voices

Up high a-bove the tree, an ea-gle I see soar-ing in the breeze.
Do do do ti la so so la so fa mi fa fa mi re do.

Piano

Up high a-bove the tree, an ea-gle I see soar-ing in the breeze.
Do do do ti la so so la so fa mi fa fa mi re do.

Up high a-bove the tree, an ea-gle I see soar-ing in the breeze.
Do do do ti la so so la so fa mi fa fa mi re do.

24 **SODA POP CANS (2-PART TREBLE)**

UNISON (OPT. 2-PART)
Piano Accompaniments

25 ALL OVER TOWN

Voices

Piano

1. Call-ing, call-ing, call-ing a-round.___ Call-ing, call-ing, all o-ver

Teacher/Leader: Singers:

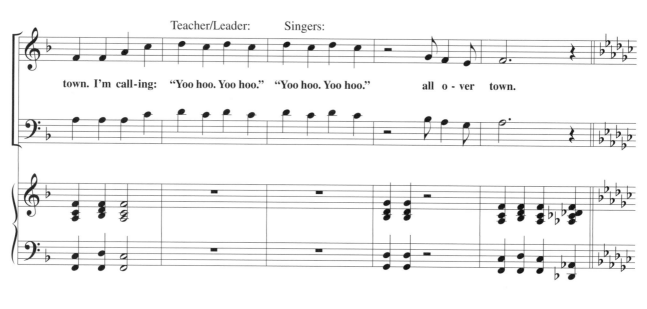

town. I'm call-ing: "Yoo hoo. Yoo hoo." "Yoo hoo. Yoo hoo." all o-ver town.

2. Laugh-ing, laugh-ing, laugh-ing a-round.___ Laugh-ing, laugh-ing, all o-ver

UNISON (OPT. 2-PART)
Piano Accompaniments

UNISON (OPT. 2-PART)
Piano Accompaniments

*improvise dance moves for 4 beats, then singers copy dance moves for next 4 beats.

FEEL THE SUBDIVISION

27 CORRAL THE CHORALE

28 TOO-RE-LOO-RE-LOO

Page 29

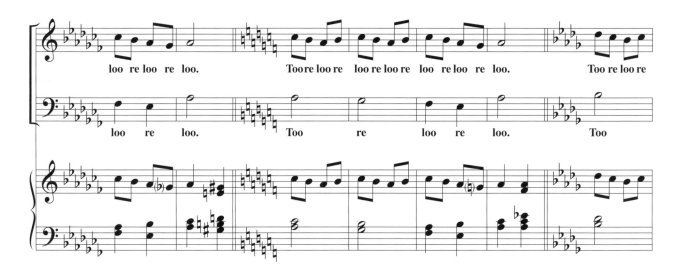

29 TAKIN' A TRIP AROUND THE WORLD

*Argentina or your choice

30 **MINER FORTY-NINER**

Page 31

Voices / Piano

Min-er For-ty-Nin-er in the mine, whose mind

is primed to find some trea-sure. Giv-en all the sto-ries I've been

told, you will find gold!

Mi - ner For - ty - Nin - er in the mine, whose mind is primed to find some trea - sure. Giv - en all the sto - ries I've been told, you will find gold!

31 MAY WE FOLLOW YOU? (2-PART)

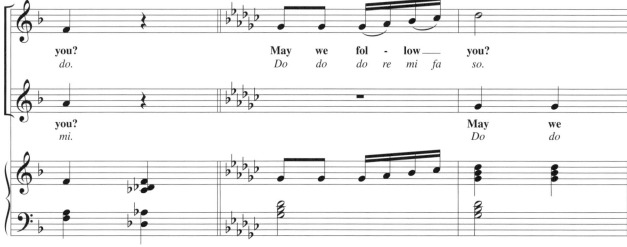

32 RING DEM BELLS

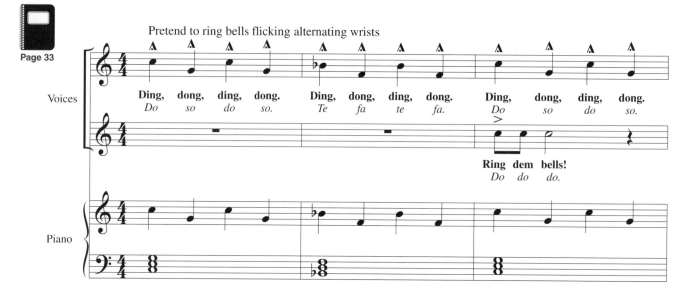
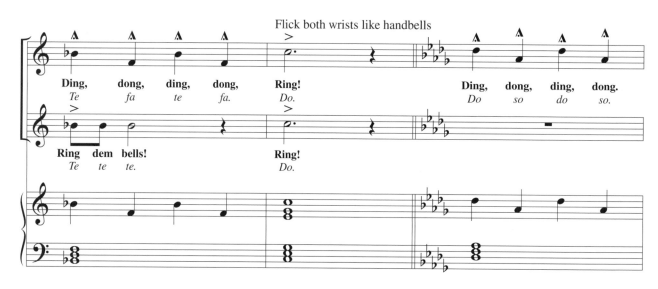

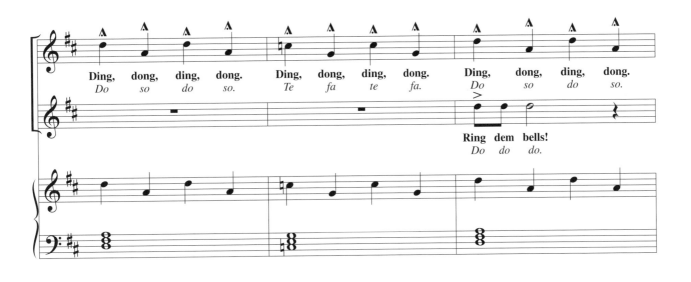

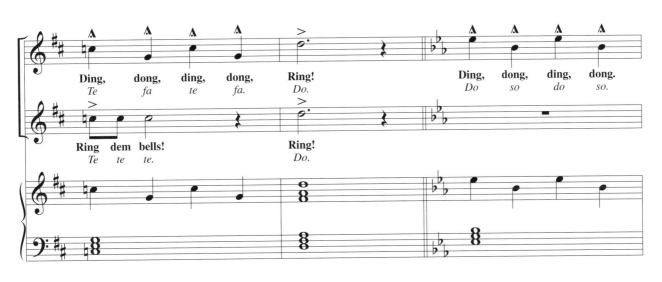

33 THE GROWING PHRASE

Voices — This is the phrase that grows and grows then ta-pers to the

Piano

end. This is the phrase that grows and grows and

grows then ta - pers to the end.

2-PART TREBLE OR MIXED
Piano Accompaniments

34 INTERVALLIC EXPANSION

2-PART TREBLE OR MIXED
Piano Accompaniments

35 TRIPLETS

36 TWO NOTE PHRASES (SIXTHS)

Page 35

2-PART TREBLE OR MIXED
Piano Accompaniments

37 TWO NOTE PHRASES (TENTHS)

Page 36

2-PART TREBLE OR MIXED
Piano Accompaniments

2-PART TREBLE OR MIXED
Piano Accompaniments

38 STAGGER YOUR BREATHING

Page 36

2-PART TREBLE OR MIXED
Piano Accompaniments

WILLOW TREE

Page 37

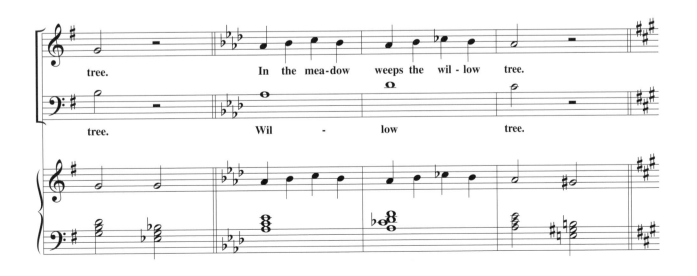

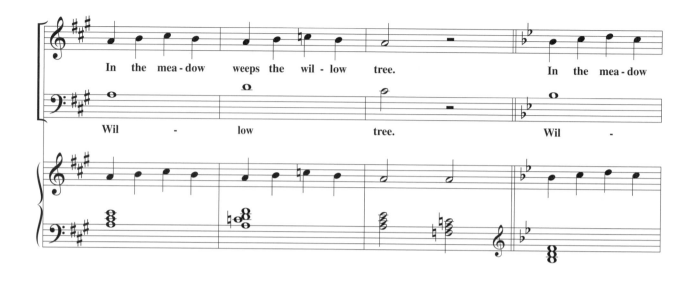

In the mea-dow weeps the wil-low tree. In the mea-dow

Wil - low tree. Wil -

weeps the wil-low tree. In the mea-dow weeps the wil-low

low tree. Wil - low

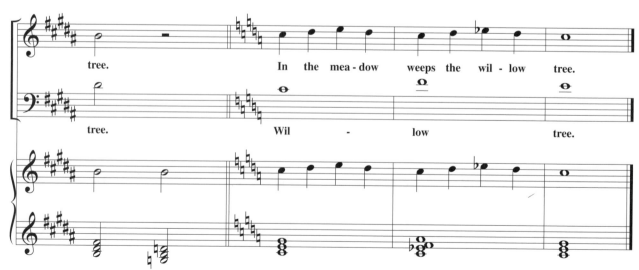

tree. In the mea-dow weeps the wil-low tree.

tree. Wil - low tree.

40 CANOE SONG

Page 37

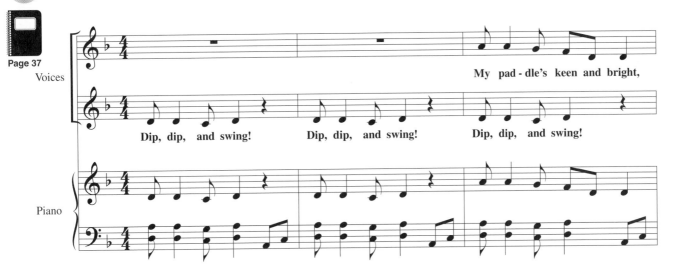

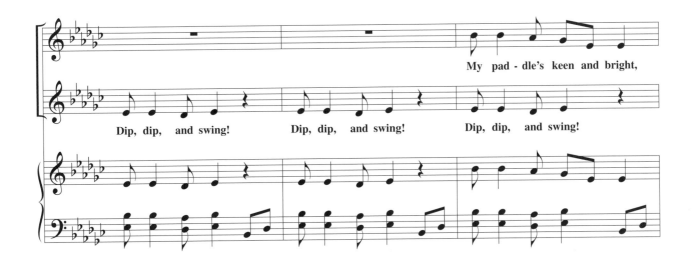

2-PART TREBLE OR MIXED
Piano Accompaniments

2-PART TREBLE OR MIXED
Piano Accompaniments

41 OH SHENANDOAH

2-PART TREBLE OR MIXED
Piano Accompaniments

42 ## SOON I WILL BE DONE

Page 38

43 DOO BAH DOO BAH

Page 39

Voices

Doo bah. Doo bah. Doo —— doo doo bah doo bah, —— doo bah.   Doo bah. Doo bah. Doo

Piano

—— doo doo bah doo bah, —— doo bah.   Doo bah. Doo bah. Doo —— doo doo bah doo bah,

—— doo bah.   Doo bah. Doo bah. Doo —— doo doo bah doo bah, —— doo bah.

44 I WILL SING THIS SONG FOR YOU (CANON)

Page 40

45 SCALE INTO HARMONY

46 SCALE WITH PEDAL POINTS

Page 42

47 COMIN' FOR TO CARRY ME HOME

Page 43

Voices

Com - in' for —— to car-ry me home. —— Com - in' for —— to

Piano

car - ry me home. —— Com - in' for —— to car - ry me home. ——

Com - in' for —— to car-ry me home. —— Com - in' for —— to car-ry me home. ——

3 OR 4-PART MIXED
Piano Accompaniments

48 ALLELUIA!

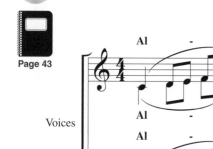

Page 43

3 OR 4-PART MIXED
Piano Accompaniments

49 ROLLING RIVER

Page 44

50 MIDNIGHT INTO MORNING

Page 45

Voices

Piano

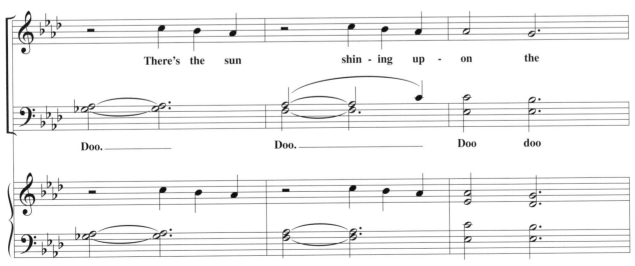

3 OR 4-PART MIXED
Piano Accompaniments

51 BEYOND THE SETTING OF THE SUN

Page 46

52 SEVEN SILVER SWANS

Page 47

SODA POP CANS (MIXED VOICES)

53

Page 48

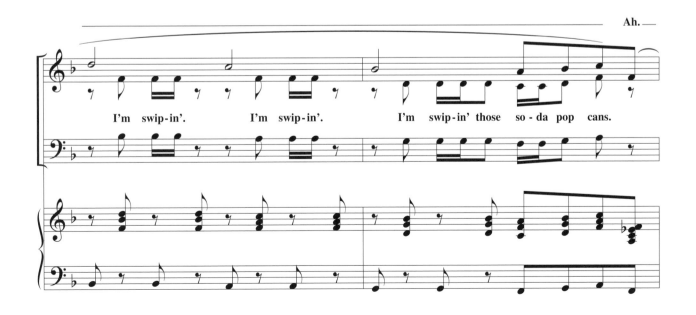

54 GETTING READY TO SING!

MULTIPLE EXPRESSION LEVELS (M.E.L.)

Encourage your singers to sing a phrase at various expression levels. As you explore singing the phrase at each level (1, 2, 3 or 4), decide which expression level best fits the style, mood and character of the phrase. Experiment with the Multiple Expression Levels concept using pieces from your choral repertoire. Explore ways in which M.E.L. can assist in making your performance more artistically expressive!

EXPRESSION LEVEL 1
- use only the eyes and eyebrows to express the mood of the music
- vary the shape of the eyes; vary the height of the eyebrows

EXPRESSION LEVEL 2
Expression Level 1 plus:
- subtle head movement that connects with phrasing, articulation, and style

EXPRESSION LEVEL 3
Expression Levels 1 and 2 plus:
- movement of the arms, shoulders, torso
- hand signals, conducting gestures, sign language, clapping, finger snapping

EXPRESSION LEVEL 4
Expression Levels 1, 2 and 3 plus:
- stepping, marching, and walking

KODÁLY/CURWEN HAND SIGNS

 do

 ti

 la

 sol

 fa

 mi

re

do

KODÁLY/CURWEN ADVANCED HAND SIGNS

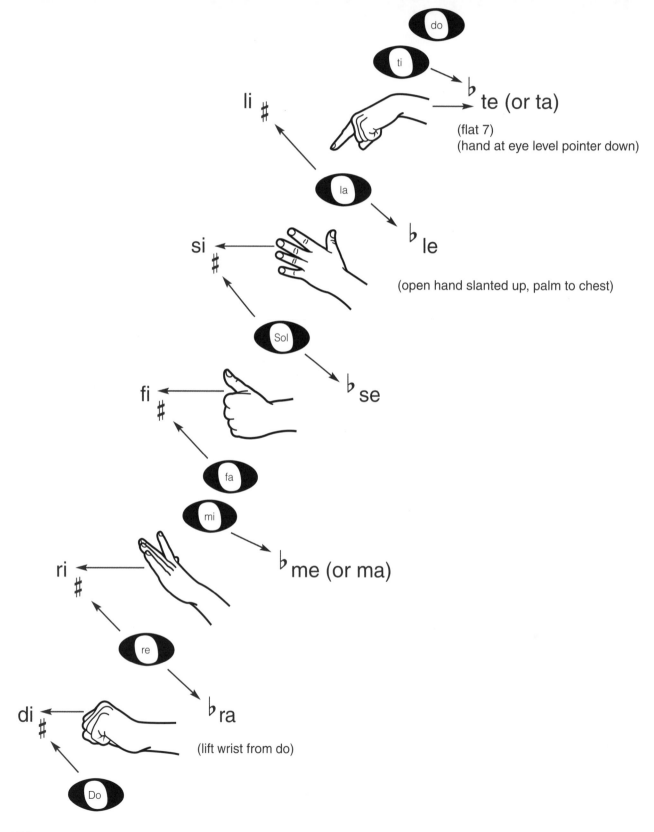

do

ti

li ♯

♭ te (or ta)
(flat 7)
(hand at eye level pointer down)

la

si
♯

♭ le

(open hand slanted up, palm to chest)

Sol

fi
♯

♭ se

fa

mi

ri
♯

♭ me (or ma)

re

di ♯

♭ ra

(lift wrist from do)

Do

KODÁLY RHYTHM SYLLABLES

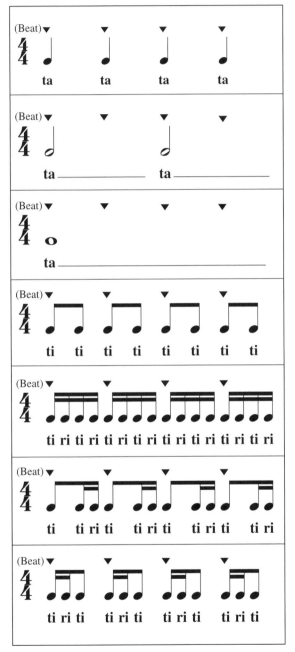

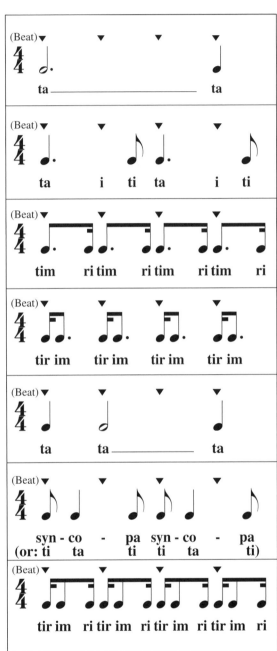

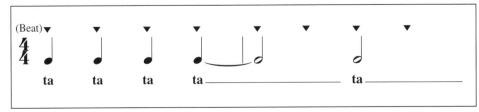

BASIC CONDUCTING PATTERNS

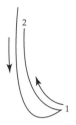

2-Beat
Pattern

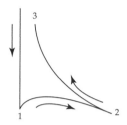

3-Beat
Pattern

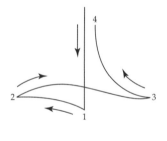

4-Beat
Pattern

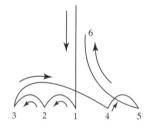

6-Beat
Pattern

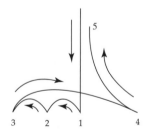

5-Beat Pattern
with accent on beat 4

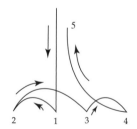

5-Beat Pattern
With accent on beat 3

National Standards for Music Education

1 Singing, alone and with others, a varied repertoire of music.

2 Performing on instruments, alone and with others, a varied repertoire of music.

3 Improvising melodies, variations, and accompaniments.

4 Composing and arranging music within specified guidelines.

5 Reading and notating music.

6 Listening to, analyzing, and describing music.

7 Evaluating music and music performances.

8 Understanding relationships between music, the other arts, and disciplines outside the arts.

9 Understanding music in relation to history and culture.

Rollo Dilworth

Rollo Dilworth is Associate Professor of Music and Director of Choral Activities and Music Education at the North Park University School of Music in Chicago, Illinois. He earned a Doctorate degree in Conducting Performance at Northwestern University and he holds undergraduate and graduate degrees from Case Western Reserve University and the University of Missouri – St. Louis, respectively.

An award-winning composer and active conductor, educator and clinician, Dilworth has taught choral music at the elementary, secondary and university levels. His performing endeavors have taken him to the continents of Europe, Asia, Africa and Australia. In addition to composing music in the choral genre, Dilworth's research interests are in the areas of African-American music and music education curriculum and instruction. Dilworth was born in 1970 in St. Louis, Missouri.